JOHN LEGEND
TWO EXTRAORDINARY PEOPLE.
MICHAEL BUBLÉ

CONNECTED LIVES™

Ariana Grande | Camila Cabello   Kacey Musgraves | Maren Morris

Ed Sheeran | Shawn Mendes   Kane Brown | Sam Hunt

Halsey | Billie Eilish   Kendrick Lamar | Travis Scott

John Legend | Michael Bublé   Nicki Minaj | Cardi B

Photo credits: page 4: Rich Polk / The Art of Elysium via Getty Images; page 5: Andrew Chin via Getty Images; page 6: Jason Merritt / Axe via Getty Images; page 7: Noam Galai via Getty Images; page 9: Glenn Pinkerton / Las Vegas News Bureau via Getty Images; page 11: Rich Lam via Getty Images; page 12: Ian Gavan / Gucci via Getty Images; page 13: Glenn Pinkerton / Las Vegas News Bureau via Getty Images; page 16: D Dipasupil via Getty Images; page 17: Neilson Barnard via Getty Images; page 18: Rick Diamond via Getty Images; page 19: Tetra Images via Getty Images; page 20: Kevin Winter via Getty Images; page 21: Michael Ochs Archives via Getty Images; page 23: Ethan Miller via Getty Images; page 24: Jon Lovette / DigitalVision via Getty Images; page 25: Bryan Bedder via Getty Images; page 28: Bennett Raglin / 2017 ESSENCE Festival via Getty Images; page 29: Glenn Pinkerton / Las Vegas News Bureau via Getty Images; page 30: Andrew Thomas / 500px Prime via Getty Images; page 31: Bryan Bedder via Getty Images; page 32: Rachel Murray / Netflix via Getty Images, Jack Berman / Moment via Getty Images; page 34: Scott Gries / American Express via Getty Images; page 35: Ethan Miller via Getty Images; page 36: Kevin Winter via Getty Images, Ricardo Tavares / 500px Prime via Getty Images; page 37: Matt Winkelmeyer / TIFF via Getty Images; page 40: Larry Marano / NFL via Getty Images; page 41: Donald Weber via Getty Images; page 42: Alberto E. Rodriguez via Getty Images; page 45: Joerg Koch via Getty Images; page 46: Alberto E. Rodriguez via Getty Images; page 48: Lisa Lake / Philly Fights Cancer via Getty Images; page 49: Ethan Miller via Getty Images; page 52: Stephen Shugerman via Getty Images; page 53: Michael Ochs Archives via Getty Images; page 54: Keystone / Hulton Archive via Getty Images; page 55: Noam Galai / Jazz At Lincoln Center via Getty Images; page 56: Kevin Winter / NARAS via Getty Images; page 58: Kevin Winter via Getty Images; page 59: Stephen Shugerman via Getty Images; page 61: Kevin Winter via Getty Images; page 62: Ben Gabbe via Getty Images; page 63: Jamie McCarthy / Breast Cancer Research Foundation via Getty Images; page 64: Rich Fury / iHeartMedia via Getty Images, Ethan Miller via Getty Images; background: Chris Wong / EyeEm via Getty Images; John Legend head shot: Rich Polk / IMDb via Getty Images; Michael Bublé head shot: Evan Agostini via Getty Images

ISBN: 978-1-68021-792-6
eBook: 978-1-64598-078-0

Printed in Malaysia

24 23 22 21 20   1 2 3 4 5

TABLE OF CONTENTS

CHAPTER 1

EARLY LIFE

WHO IS JOHN LEGEND?

John Legend is an R&B singer and songwriter. He was born on December 28, 1978. His parents named him John Roger Stephens. The star had humble beginnings. Springfield, Ohio, is where his family lived. In Springfield, many people were struggling to earn money. John's parents had to work hard to survive.

WHO IS MICHAEL BUBLÉ?

Three years before John, Michael Steven Bublé was born. His birthday is September 9, 1975. Like John, he grew up to become a famous singer and songwriter. But Michael's style is jazz rather than R&B. His family lived in Burnaby, British Columbia. The city is on the west coast of Canada, just outside of Vancouver. Jobs at sea are common there. Michael's father worked in the fishing industry.

Ronald Stephens

FAMILY AT HOME

John's parents are Ronald and Phyllis Stephens. Ronald worked in a factory that built farm equipment and trucks. He had served in the National Guard. Phyllis was a seamstress. She sewed clothes for a living. The couple had four children. Ronald Jr. was the oldest. John was born next. Then came a third boy, Vaughn. He also grew up to be a singer. Phyllis (Missy) was the baby and only girl.

AWAY AT SEA

Michael's father, Lewis, had a dangerous job. He was a salmon fisherman. Lewis often spent months away at sea. His wife, Amber, stayed home with their three children. Like John, Michael grew up with siblings at home. He is the oldest, with two younger sisters. Their names are Brandee and Crystal. Brandee became a children's book author. Crystal is an actress.

MUSICAL SIBLINGS

Musical talent seems to run in some families. Many famous singers have brothers or sisters who have also tried to make it in the music industry. One example is Beyoncé's sister Solange. She got her start as a backup dancer for her sister's group, Destiny's Child. Later, she released her own music. Other siblings have worked together to form family bands, such as the Jonas Brothers.

Solange Knowles

LIFE LESSONS

John's mother homeschooled him for some of elementary school. He also attended the public school in town. His parents didn't want him and his siblings to learn just school subjects. Life lessons were important too. The family had books "that were about what it means to be hardworking, determined, loving, patient . . . and how to succeed in the right way," John told *InStyle* magazine.

Springfield, Ohio

HELP FROM GRANDPARENTS

Michael's grandparents helped his mom raise the kids. Demetrio (Mitch) and Yolanda had emigrated from Italy. Michael was close to both of them. His grandmother taught him how to cook Italian food. He had a special bond with his grandfather. The singer explained to the *Sun*, "He was my best friend growing up." Jazz music was one interest they shared. Like John, Michael was learning about subjects that would help him as an adult.

GOSPEL AND HISTORY

One of John's main interests while growing up was gospel music. His whole family was involved in music at their church. "I was in choir rehearsals every week as a kid, and I took over the choir when I was older," he told *People* magazine.

John also loved history. He explained to the *Wall Street Journal*, "My parents used to take me to the library, and that's where I would read with pride about Martin Luther King and Frederick Douglass and Harriet Tubman." This interest has stayed with him throughout his life.

GOSPEL MUSIC

Gospel music got its start in Christian churches in the 19th century. It features strong vocals accompanied by a piano or an organ. Other instruments were added in some churches. African American singers played a large role in its development. Like many other artists, John began singing in church. Aretha Franklin, Beyoncé, and Usher all started out singing gospel music.

HOCKEY AND JAZZ

Growing up, Michael loved hockey. He played with his friends whenever possible. Secretly, he had a dream. It was to be a professional hockey player. Michael wanted to play for the National Hockey League (NHL) team in nearby Vancouver. "I went to every single Canucks home game as a kid," he told NHL.com.

When not playing hockey, Michael was listening to music. Usually jazz was playing. Sometimes he would sing to himself when no one was around. His other secret dream was to become a performer.

TEACHER SUPPORT

When John was ten, his parents divorced. After that, his mother went through a difficult time. The kids were raised by their dad, Ronald. Divorce was hard on John and his siblings. John had several teachers who helped. He told *People*, "All of these people took extra time to show me that they cared." School could have been difficult. His teachers didn't let that happen. They "saw my potential and sparked my passion," he wrote in *HuffPost*.

A ROUGH TIME

Michael's school experience was different from John's. He did not enjoy high school. "I didn't really fit into any group," he commented in the short documentary *Michael Bublé's Day Off*. As a teenager, Michael wore shirts with the names of rock and heavy metal bands on them. This made him stand out. "I wasn't part of the super-cool popular crowd, and even though I loved sports, I wasn't a jock," he wrote in his book *Onstage Offstage*. Michael was an average student who got bored easily.

OFF TO COLLEGE

John loved learning. He skipped two grades and graduated from high school at age 16. The school named him salutatorian of his class. That means his grades were the second highest overall. Several colleges had accepted John, including Harvard University. A scholarship led him to the University of Pennsylvania, in Philadelphia. The city had a great music scene. Many musicians lived there. This was an exciting place for John to be.

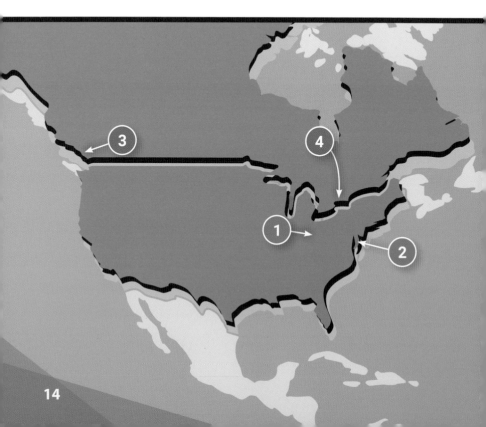

SALMON FISHING

As a teen, Michael worked a summer job. At age 14, he started joining his dad for two to three months of salmon fishing. It was "the most deadly physical work I'll ever know," he told the *Times*. Sometimes they worked for 20 hours without stopping. Michael did it every summer for six years. Fishing taught him how to work hard. After high school, he didn't go to college. Instead, Michael wanted to focus on his dream of becoming a singer.

JOHN LEGEND

1. **Springfield, Ohio:** This is John's hometown. His whole family was involved in the church choir here.

2. **New York City, New York:** John moved here after college. He worked as a consultant during the day and played music at night.

MICHAEL BUBLÉ

3. **Burnaby, British Columbia:** Michael grew up here. As an adult, he built a house here.

4. **Toronto, Ontario:** A performance at a corporate event led to Michael's big break.

CHAPTER 2

INTRO TO MUSIC

PIANO LESSONS

John's introduction to music came at a very young age. In 1982, John was four years old. He wanted to play piano. His grandmother started to teach him. She played the organ at their church. His father played the drums. John's brothers were also drummers. Phyllis directed the choir and sang. When John was seven years old, he joined the church choir too.

SING THE WAY HOME

Unlike John's family, no one in Michael's family played an instrument. They enjoyed singing at home. It was just for fun, though. Michael's father had taught him his first song. This was the family's address. "He knew that by singing it, I'd remember it," Michael wrote in *Onstage Offstage*. From the age of two, Michael would entertain his family. He danced and sang around the living room. As a teenager, he spent hours singing alone in his room.

A MIX OF MUSIC

Music helped distract John after his parents' divorce. He listened to a mix of old and new music. Classical music might get him through one day. Hip-hop got him through the next. As a teenager, he bought many different types of records. John's father loved Motown and soul music. This is what he played all the time at home. Jazz was another favorite. Ronald introduced John to artists like Nina Simone and Nat King Cole.

JAZZ INSTRUMENTS

The first jazz bands were made up of brass instruments, such as trumpets and trombones. Later, some musicians sang with just a piano to accompany them. Others were backed by small orchestras. These included string instruments, such as violins, as well as brass. Drums also played an important part, helping to keep the rhythm.

EARLY JAZZ INFLUENCE

Jazz was an even bigger part of Michael's life. His grandfather had a huge collection of old records. They were from the 1930s and 1940s. When Michael was five years old, he started listening to them. He heard singers like Frank Sinatra and Dean Martin. These performers had Italian roots, just like Michael's family. His grandfather felt a special connection to these performers. "He was the one who opened me up to a whole world of music," Michael wrote on his website.

WHEN YOU KNOW, YOU KNOW

"As soon as I started singing and playing, I wanted to be doing it on TV," John told the *Guardian*. From a young age, he knew music would be a big part of his life. John wrote an essay at age 15. It talked about his life goals. "I want to become an artist, work in the music business, be successful and use that success to be a leader in other ways," John said he wrote. Years later, he had reached all those goals.

Bing Crosby

THE SURPRISE SINGER

Like John, Michael had dreamed about
becoming a performer since he was a child.
"I wanted to be a singer and I knew that [jazz] was the
music that I wanted to sing," he said on his website. His
family, however, had no idea. When Michael was 13,
Bing Crosby's classic recording of "White Christmas"
came on the radio. He started singing along. The family
was shocked. No one had known how good his voice was.

COUNTERPARTS

At 16, John left home to attend the University of Pennsylvania. His major was English. He focused on African American literature. Music was still a part of his life. In college, he directed and sang in an *a cappella* group. It was called Counterparts. "John was shy, smart, focused, and he had the best voice any of us had ever heard," said his friend Ty Stiklorius in the *Wall Street Journal*.

WHAT IS *A CAPPELLA*?

A *cappella* is music that is sung without any instruments to back it up. In the late 19th century, *a cappella* groups started to form on college campuses. Since the 1980s, these groups have become even more popular. Competitions between schools take place. Some singers in these groups perform drum noises. They can sound almost like the real thing. The TV show *Glee*, which was about an *a cappella* group, got many people interested in singing. The year after it came out, 43 percent of music teachers said more students had joined their choirs.

CAREER CHOICE

Unlike John, Michael didn't go to college. As a teenager, he had started voice lessons. His grandfather paid for them. Grandpa Mitch wanted to help any way he could. Michael still loved hockey, but he was better at singing. "If I was any good at hockey, I probably wouldn't be singing right now," the star told NHL.com.

Philadelphia, Pennsylvania

KEEPING BUSY

While in college, John also directed a church's gospel choir. It was in Scranton, Pennsylvania. Every weekend, he drove two hours to get there. Then he returned to school in Philadelphia. "It was a great time in my life," he said in an interview. Still, his friends worried about him. Music and school were exhausting him.

FAMILY SUPPORT

Michael was also staying busy with music. He had started singing in restaurants around town during his free time. His grandfather wanted to help. Mitch offered plumbing services to anyone who would hire his grandson. On the TV show *60 Minutes*, Michael said his grandfather told them, "You let him up onstage and I'm gonna go and fix your hot water heater."

PHILADELPHIA AND BEYOND

Philadelphia had lots of places where John could play gigs. Sometimes he would play piano and sing at clubs or restaurants. Other times, he would play backup for different singers. Soon, he started traveling farther to perform. One weekend, he might stay in Philadelphia. The following week, he might travel to New York City for a gig. John was starting to make a name for himself. Usually the singer performed R&B songs. R&B stands for rhythm and blues. This music combines pop, hip-hop, and jazz elements.

LOCAL GIGS

While John was playing gigs in cities on the East Coast, Michael was trying to make it as a singer in Vancouver. Often, his performances were just background noise. He sang for people eating in restaurants. They "cared more about their food" than his singing, he told the *Guardian*.

When Michael was a teen, he won a local talent contest. An agent named Beverly Delich had organized it. Michael had to be disqualified though. He was a year too young for the contest. However, Delich was impressed by the singer. She had plans for him.

PARALLEL LIVES

Born in the U.S.

Sang gospel

Took piano lessons

Wanted to sing from a
young age

Grandparent played an important role
in musical education

Born in Canada

Sang jazz

Took voice lessons

CHAPTER 3

RISE TO SUCCESS

EVERYTHING IS EVERYTHING

In 1998, a big opportunity came up for John in New York. He auditioned to play piano for Lauryn Hill's album *The Miseducation of Lauryn Hill*. She hired him to play on her song "Everything Is Everything." The song came out the next year. It was a top 40 hit. At the time, John was still in college. People at his school were impressed. "I went back to college and I was the man after that," he joked in an interview with Yahoo!

ON HIS WAY

Delich, the agent, told Michael to try out for the British Columbia Youth Talent Search. In 1993, he entered and won. "It was an auditorium of like 2,000 people and everybody stood. He was so good," Delich told Charged.fm. Michael asked her to be his manager. At first, she wasn't sure. There didn't seem to be a big market for a teenager who sang jazz. Finally, in 1995, she agreed.

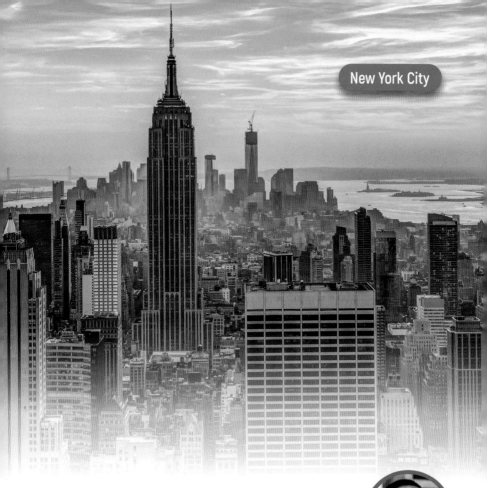

NEW YORK CITY

John graduated college in 1999. Then he moved to New York City. He worked at a consulting company. His job was to help businesses become more effective. It wasn't what he wanted to do for the rest of his life. At night, he played piano and sang at clubs around the city. "I couldn't shake my passion for music," John wrote in an essay for CNN.

WORKING HARD

Michael was working any music-related job he could get. He sang at talent shows, malls, and clubs. For a while, he even worked as a singing telegram messenger. His job was to deliver musical messages to people. In 1996, the TV show *The X-Files* hired him. On one episode, he played a submarine crew member. Then he got fired. Someone had seen him eat a hot dog off a table of food meant for the stars of the show.

NEW NAME

While working in Manhattan, John recorded two CDs independently. The first was a demo that he made in 2000. A year later, he came out with *Live at Jimmy's Uptown*. He sold the CDs at his shows.

In 2002, John quit his consulting job. He wanted to pursue his music career. Around this time, he also started using a stage name. The singer called himself "John Legend." A friend had told him he sounded like "one of the legends."

TRYING TO MAKE IT

Michael recorded his first independent album in 1996. It was called *First Dance*. There were six songs on it. In 1997, Michael played Elvis Presley in the musical *Red Rock Diner* in Vancouver. The next year, he was cast in another musical, *Forever Swing*. It toured around Canada. In late 1999, the show ended its tour in Toronto. Michael decided to stay. Moving to a bigger city might help him make it in music.

INDEPENDENT ALBUMS

Getting signed to a major record label is difficult. The music industry is very competitive. Often, artists need to have built an audience before they get signed. One way to do this is to put out an independent album.

Musicians pay for the album themselves. Renting a studio for recording is the first step. Then they must advertise and sell the record. Social media helps with this. Artists can sell CDs at concerts too. Michael and John sold their CDs at gigs.

MEETING KANYE

In 2001, John talked to a college friend. The friend wanted to introduce him to someone. His cousin had just moved to New York. He was going to work on Jay-Z's new album. John agreed to meet him. Soon, he connected with the young producer. His name was Kanye West. West was just getting started in music too. "People didn't even know he could rap really yet," John said at the Tribeca Film Festival. The two helped each other on songs. They were both putting demo albums together to send to record labels.

Kanye West

THE PRIME MINISTER

In 2000, Michael was hired to sing at an event in Toronto. The performer had been thinking about giving up on music. At the event, Michael McSweeney heard him. He had worked for Brian Mulroney, the former Canadian prime minister.

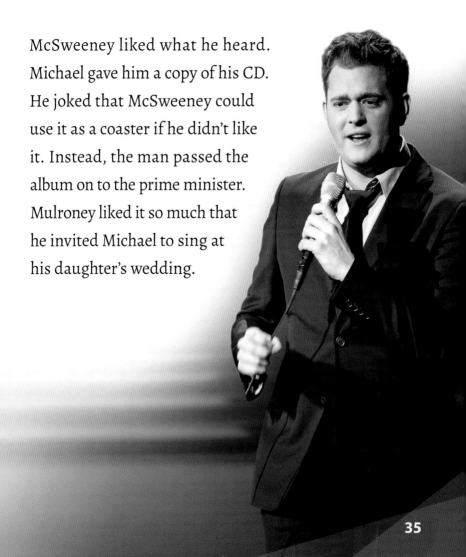

McSweeney liked what he heard. Michael gave him a copy of his CD. He joked that McSweeney could use it as a coaster if he didn't like it. Instead, the man passed the album on to the prime minister. Mulroney liked it so much that he invited Michael to sing at his daughter's wedding.

GROWING CROWDS

It was 2003. John peeked out at the audience. He was about to play a concert at a small club in New York. There must have been 300 or 400 people there. The singer couldn't believe it. Just a few years earlier, he was happy to have 50 or 60 people hear him perform. His friend Kanye had been the opening act. Now it was John's turn to take the stage.

David Foster

"MACK THE KNIFE"

The wedding of Mulroney's daughter was a high-profile event. It was the most important performance so far in Michael's career. He came bursting out on stage with the 1950s hit "Mack the Knife." People couldn't take their eyes off of him.

After the performance, Michael was introduced to a wedding guest. The man was music producer David Foster. He had produced albums and songs for many stars. They included Madonna, Celine Dion, and many others.

GET LIFTED

In 2004, Kanye helped John get signed to
Columbia Records. This was a huge step. John
had been trying to sign with a major record label since
1998. His debut album, *Get Lifted*, came out the same
year he was signed. "Ordinary People" was a big hit
from the album. He won three Grammy Awards. One
was for Best R&B Album. John also won the award for
Best New Artist.

ALMOST THERE

Foster didn't know if people would like
Michael's music. Still, he recognized the
singer's talent. If Michael could come up with the
money for his first studio album, Foster would help
make it. Each track would cost $100,000. Michael
found someone who would loan him the money. The
producer signed him to his label, 143 Records. In 2003,
the album *Michael Bublé* came out. Michael won New
Artist of the Year in 2004. This was at the Juno Awards.
These awards are given to Canadian musical artists.

CAREER MILESTONES

1998
John plays piano on Lauryn Hill's award-winning album.

2000
Michael is discovered by the former prime minister of Canada. He meets big-name producer David Foster.

2003
Michael's first album, *Michael Bublé*, is released. Later that year, *Let It Snow* comes out.

2004
John's debut album, *Get Lifted*, comes out.

2006
John wins his first Grammy Award.

2007
Michael takes home his first Grammy Award.

2013
Michael's album *To Be Loved* hits number one on the Billboard 200 chart.

2014
John's song "All of Me" hits number one.

2016
The fifth studio album by John, *Darkness and Light*, is released.

2016
Michael's ninth album, *Nobody but Me*, comes out.

2018
John releases *A Legendary Christmas*.

2018
Michael's album ♥ (*Love*) comes out.

2019
John is the winning coach on season 16 of *The Voice*.

2019
Michael stars in a Super Bowl LIII commercial for Bubly water.

CHAPTER 4

STARDOM

BIG-LEAGUE PERFORMER

John was becoming more popular. In 2006, he
performed at Super Bowl XL. He got to sing with
one of his idols, Stevie Wonder. Many of the songs
were R&B classics that John had grown up hearing.
That same year, he sang at the National Basketball
Association All-Star Game.
John also performed at
the Major League Baseball
All-Star Game. People were
excited about his music.

IT'S TIME

The "Canadian Sinatra" was soon releasing number-one
albums and songs. Michael's second album was *It's Time*.
A track from it called "Home" hit number one on the
Billboard Adult Contemporary chart in 2005. He won his
first Grammy for *Call Me Irresponsible* in 2007. Many were
surprised at Michael's popularity.
"People have certain ideas of what
they think you should be, and I
have fought that . . . my whole
life," he told the *Evening Standard*.

BREAKING INTO THE MOVIES

John's music wasn't just popular at concerts and sporting events. In 2012, he wrote a song called "Who Did That to You?" It was for the film *Django Unchained*. The song explores the film's themes of struggle and racism. He told *Rolling Stone*, "These are things that I have thought about for years."

In 2016, John played a bandleader in the movie *La La Land*. His character thought it was important to experiment with music. In many ways, John identified with him. "As much as you can be influenced by the past . . . it's important to carry that forward and create something new," he told *Entertainment Weekly*.

OLYMPIC GAMES CEREMONIES

The 2010 Winter Olympic Games were held in Vancouver, British Columbia. Many Canadian celebrities performed in the opening and closing ceremonies. Michael was one of them. He also carried the Olympic torch. It is a big honor to be chosen to do this. For the closing ceremonies, Michael was dressed as a Mountie. Mounties are Canadian police. He sang "The Maple Leaf Forever," a traditional Canadian song.

LOVE IN THE FUTURE

John released his fourth studio album in 2013. It was called *Love in the Future*. The album was number four on the Billboard 200 chart the week it came out. A track called "All of Me" became a big hit. In 2014, the song reached number one on the Hot 100 chart. John wrote the song for his future wife. Her name is Chrissy Teigen. She starred in the music video of the song with John.

GRAMMY AWARDS

Every year, the Recording Academy gives out Grammy Awards. People in the music industry, such as singers, musicians, and producers, can win them. Originally, they were called the Gramophone Awards. A gramophone was an early type of record player.

Some of the awards are Album of the Year and Song of the Year. Music from any genre can win these. Other awards are given out for different genres, such as pop or jazz. As of 2019, John has won ten awards and Michael has won four.

CRAZY LOVE

Like John, Michael found inspiration from his love life. "Haven't Met You Yet" was written for his then-girlfriend. Her name was Luisana Lopilato. Michael told PopEater that the song was about "everyone's dream of finding a relationship and love." Like Teigen, Lopilato appeared in the song's music video with Michael. The couple married two years later.

EGOT

By 2017, John had won Grammys and an Oscar (Academy Award). That year, he also won a Tony Award for a Broadway show he had co-produced. In 2018, John starred in *Jesus Christ Superstar Live in Concert* on NBC. He also co-produced the show. It won several Emmy Awards. This put John in a small group of people who have won Emmy, Grammy, Oscar, and Tony awards. Winning all four is called an EGOT. John was the first African American man to achieve this.

HOLLYWOOD WALK OF FAME

Over two decades, Michael went from a teenager performing in talent shows to an international star. By 2018, he had gone on several world tours. His concerts had sold out in the U.S. and in the United Kingdom. Like John, Michael had won many awards for music. This included four Grammys. In November 2018, Michael received a star on the Hollywood Walk of Fame.

HOLLYWOOD STARS

The Hollywood Walk of Fame opened in 1960. It runs down Hollywood Boulevard in Hollywood, California, passing the famous Grauman's Chinese Theatre. Once they have become successful, actors, musicians, and others are invited to place their handprints next to a star with their name on it. Michael Bublé was given the honor in 2018. He joined his heroes Elvis Presley and Frank Sinatra. Other recent stars include Mandy Moore, Pink, Carrie Underwood, and Lin-Manuel Miranda.

CHARITY WORK

Growing up in Springfield made John think about education. Almost half of his classmates had dropped out before graduating. As an adult, he wanted to help. Becoming a father also showed him how important education is. The singer supports Teach for America and the Education Equality Project. They both help provide opportunities in poor communities.

FAMILY IN CRISIS

By 2016, Michael and his wife had two children. Then
the family got devastating news. Their oldest son, Noah,
was diagnosed with liver cancer. In order to focus on his
family, Michael quit music. His son had to go through
lots of treatments. Two years later, Noah's cancer was
in remission. Going back on tour in 2019 was a way for
Michael to thank his fans for their support.

THE VOICE

John announced in 2018 that he was joining the cast of *The Voice*. He would be a coach on the reality show. The other coaches were Adam Levine, Blake Shelton, and Kelly Clarkson. All are famous artists. "I'm so excited to discover talented singers and help them make the most of their gift," John said in a statement. The next year, he coached Maelyn Jarmon to win the season.

TOP BILLBOARD 200 ALBUM CHART

● JOHN LEGEND STUDIO ALBUMS

#		Album	Date
#4	♪	Get Lifted	12/2004
#3	♪	Once Again	10/2006
#4	♪	Evolver	10/2008
#4	♪	Love in the Future	9/2013
#15	♪	Darkness and Light	12/2016
#5	♪	A Legendary Christmas	10/2018

LOVE

The album ❤ (pronounced *Love*) came out in 2018. It was Michael's first album in two years. He hadn't released anything while his son was sick. When announcing the album, he explained why it took so long. "I wanted to spend all my time with my wife and kids," Michael said. "You learn a lot about life and what's important and what matters," he added.

● MICHAEL BUBLÉ STUDIO ALBUMS

#47	Michael Bublé	2/2003
#7	It's Time	2/2005
#1	Call Me Irresponsible	5/2007
#1	Crazy Love	10/2009
#1	Christmas	10/2011
#1	To Be Loved	4/2013
#2	Nobody but Me	10/2016
#2	❤ (Love)	11/2018

CHAPTER 5

INFLUENCES AND COLLABORATIONS

STRONG FOUNDATION

John's biggest influence growing up was gospel music. "That was the foundation of my career," he told *People*. "I wouldn't be where I am without playing gospel music in church." His grandmother was a big inspiration too. She was his first music teacher. "I think my first big mentor is my grandmother," he explained to *Spin*. "[I] got to see her play all the time and it still influences the way I play now."

Ronald Stephens

Marjorie Stephens

ALL THAT JAZZ

Michael's love of music also began with his family. His grandfather's record collection helped him become an international star. He told *Applause* magazine, "Although I like rock 'n' roll and modern music, the first time my granddad played me the Mills Brothers, something magical happened." The Mills Brothers were a jazz quartet. They were popular in the 1930s and 1940s.

The Mills Brothers

R&B ROOTS

R&B was a big part of John's musical life too. He grew up listening to Motown singers. Some were Stevie Wonder and Marvin Gaye. Like Michael, John was also influenced by jazz singers of the past. Another inspiration is U2. John admires lead singer Bono's charity work. He's "done a lot of great work and obviously made a lot of great hit music at the same time," John said on SiriusXM.

JAZZ STANDARDS AND CROONERS

Jazz standards are important songs from the 1940s and 1950s. These songs were often performed by crooners. A crooner was typically a male singer. He sang love songs in a soft voice. Famous examples are Frank Sinatra, Dean Martin, and Tony Bennett.

Many women sang this type of music too, although they were not called crooners. Ella Fitzgerald was one of the most popular. She was called the "First Lady of Song."

Dean Martin

MODERN JAZZ

Much of Michael's style comes from jazz classics. His albums have been inspired by these popular songs. He gives them new elements. Modern lyrics also update his classic sound.

Another influence is the New Orleans singer Harry Connick Jr. He rose to fame in the 1990s. A lot of the songs he performed were jazz classics. People saw Michael as following in his footsteps. They sang similar music.

Harry Connick Jr.

Alicia Keys

IN THE BACKGROUND

John's first collaborations were as a background vocalist. Playing piano as a session musician helped him get his start. Session musicians play instruments for singers while they are recording music. This work gave him the chance to meet artists like Alicia Keys and Lauryn Hill. John wrote songs for other artists too. One was "I Want You" for Janet Jackson.

SONGWRITING

Michael's first performances were as a solo artist. He didn't play any instruments like John did. Songwriting came later for him. He told *Express,* "I've never learned to read or write music, but I just love melodies and I write from a very emotional place." Eventually, Michael cowrote several songs with Amy Foster and pianist Alan Chang. Amy Foster is the daughter of producer David Foster. Chang has also worked as Michael's music director.

MOTOWN

Motown was one of John's biggest influences. It was a record label that started in 1959. The name came from combining *motor* and *town*. This was a nickname for Detroit, Michigan, where the label was founded. Detroit was called "motor city." Many factories that made cars were there.

Over the years, the label promoted artists who were African American. Some Motown musicians and groups are Stevie Wonder, the Jackson 5, and the Supremes.

COMMON

One important collaboration for John was with the rapper Common. Together, he and John wrote the song "Glory." It was for the 2014 film *Selma*. The movie is about Martin Luther King Jr. and voting rights. Their song won an Academy Award, a Grammy, and a Golden Globe. John told *Entertainment Weekly*, "I thought [the film] was such brilliant, brilliant work, and I was so proud to be affiliated with it."

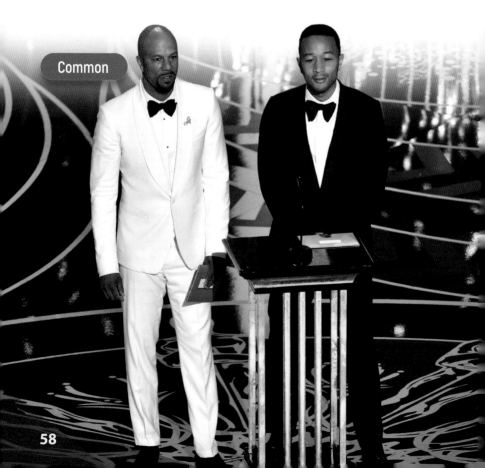

Common

Tony Bennett

TONY BENNETT

In 2006, Michael got the chance to sing with one of his idols. Tony Bennett is a crooner. His career started in the 1950s. Bennett released an album called *Duets: An American Classic*. On it, he sang duets with modern artists. Michael recorded "Just in Time" with Bennett. John also performed a duet on the CD. Five years later, Bennett and Michael sang the jazz classic "Don't Get Around Much Anymore" for the album *Duets II*. Lady Gaga sang on this album too.

KANYE AND THE ROOTS

John's work with Kanye West has helped both of their careers. He helped West write songs for a demo tape. The first album West produced on his G.O.O.D. Music label was John's *Get Lifted*.

In 2010, the star worked on an album with The Roots, an R&B group. *Wake Up!* hit number eight on the Billboard 200 chart. Later, it won three Grammy Awards, including Best R&B Album.

COVERS AND DUETS

In his career, Michael has had success with both old and new songs. Before writing his own music, he started out doing covers. One was his 2003 version of the song "For Once in My Life." This was influenced by the 1968 Stevie Wonder version of the song. Stevie Wonder inspired both John and Michael. The songs Michael performs also lend themselves easily to duets. Over the years, he has performed with Boyz II Men, Mariah Carey, and Shania Twain.

STEVIE WONDER
SHARED INFLUENCE

Both John and Michael have been inspired by Stevie Wonder. The Motown musician and singer had his first number-one hit song in 1963. He was just 13 years old. Here are more details about the best-selling artist.

Early Life

- Born May 13, 1950, in Michigan
- Born prematurely and became blind almost at birth
- First sang with a church choir
- Taught himself several instruments by age ten

Combination of Musical Styles

- R&B
- Funk
- Rock 'n' roll
- Pop
- Soul
- Jazz

Famous Songs

- "For Once in My Life" (1968)
- "Signed, Sealed, Delivered I'm Yours" (1970)
- "You Are the Sunshine of My Life" (1972)

Stevie Wonder

BECOMING A LEGEND

A Christmas album was something John had always wanted to do. In 2018, he came out with *A Legendary Christmas*. Many of his favorite artists inspired the album. "The style palette is Nat King Cole, Stevie Wonder, Marvin Gaye," John told the *Wall Street Journal*. One song, "What Christmas Means to Me," features Stevie Wonder playing the harmonica. This was an important album to John. He said, "It just feels like this is what I was made to do."

THROUGH THE NIGHT

For Michael, ♥ (*Love*) is a thank you to his fans. "Help Me Make It Through the Night" is an important song on the album. Many artists had covered it before, including Elvis. Michael wanted to perform it as a duet. He chose Loren Allred to sing it with him. Her voice had caught his attention when he saw *The Greatest Showman*. Normally, the song was sad. But Michael changed the ending to make it hopeful. He told *Entertainment Weekly*, "Making the music I love has become more joy than I ever hoped it could be."

Loren Allred

CONNECTED LIVES

Both artists have worked their way to the top of their genres. The path hasn't always been easy. John and Michael each get to make the music they want to make. Music is a fulfilling part of their lives.

TAKE A LOOK INSIDE

KACEY MUSGRAVES

TWO EXTRAORDINARY PEOPLE.

MAREN MORRIS

CHAPTER 1

EARLY LIFE

WHO IS KACEY MUSGRAVES?

Kacey Musgraves is a country music singer and songwriter. Her birthday is August 21, 1988. She was born in Golden, Texas. This is a small town about 75 miles east of Dallas. Around 200 people live there. Many of them work on farms. Until Kacey became a star, Golden was best known for growing sweet potatoes. Every year there is a festival to celebrate the crop.

WHO IS MAREN MORRIS?

About 100 miles west of Golden is the city of Arlington, Texas. Maren Morris was born there on April 10, 1990. Like Kacey, she became a singer and songwriter. Arlington is much bigger than Golden. It has a population of around 400,000. The big cities of Dallas and Fort Worth are nearby. Other musicians have come from Arlington. Pentatonix, an *a cappella* group, started there.

4

5

GETTING ON TV

In 2007, Kacey competed on the fifth season of *Nashville Star*. This was a country music reality TV show. The singer was eliminated in the third episode. She came in seventh place. "I didn't really know what I was getting myself into," she explained to *The Fader*. Even though Kacey didn't win, she learned a lot from the experience. "I was very young and figuring myself out musically and personally," she told Yahoo! Music.

REALITY SHOW REJECTIONS

In her late teens, Maren auditioned for several reality shows. She tried out for *American Idol*, *Nashville Star*, *The Voice*, and *America's Got Talent*. All of them turned her down. "I was heartbroken at the time," she told the *Dallas Observer*. Maren was getting tired of performing at shows around Texas. "Eventually, I wanted a new challenge," she added. It was time for the next step.

PARALLEL LIVES

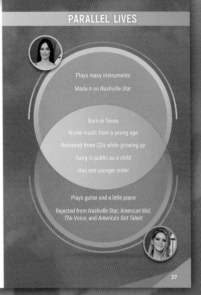

Plays many instruments
Made it on *Nashville Star*

Born in Texas
Wrote music from a young age
Released three CDs while growing up
Sang in public as a child
Has one younger sister

Plays guitar and a little piano
Rejected from *Nashville Star*, *American Idol*, *The Voice*, and *America's Got Talent*

OH, WHAT A WORLD

In 2018, Kacey had several TV appearances. She sang on *The Late Show with Stephen Colbert*. *Saturday Night Live (SNL)* had her as the musical guest in May. The star performed two songs from *Golden Hour*. Kacey also had a small appearance in the film *Wild Rose*. Her success kept growing. Later in 2018, she launched her Oh, What a World Tour. It went to cities across the U.S. as well as to Europe. The tour continued into 2019.

GIRL: THE WORLD TOUR

Like Kacey, Maren had performed on TV. In 2016, she was the musical guest on *SNL*. The TV show *NCIS: New Orleans* also hired her for a small role.

In 2019, Maren went on tour to promote her new album. Girl: The World Tour had dates in Mexico, Europe, Australia, and North America.

TOP BILLBOARD HOT 100 SINGLES

KACEY MUSGRAVES

#	Title	Date
#60	Merry Go 'Round	9/2012
#63	Follow Your Arrow	10/2013
#98	Rainbow	2/2019

MAREN MORRIS

#	Title	Date
#50	My Church	1/2016
#5	The Middle featuring Zedd, Grey	1/2018
#44	Girl	3/2019

FOR MORE TITLES AND INFORMATION $\longrightarrow$

CONNECTED LIVES™

ARIANA GRANDE
TWO EXTRAORDINARY PEOPLE.
CAMILA CABELLO
9781680217957

ED SHEERAN
TWO EXTRAORDINARY PEOPLE.
SHAWN MENDES
9781680217896

HALSEY
TWO EXTRAORDINARY PEOPLE.
BILLIE EILISH
9781680217919

JOHN LEGEND
TWO EXTRAORDINARY PEOPLE.
MICHAEL BUBLÉ
9781680217926

KACEY MUSGRAVES
TWO EXTRAORDINARY PEOPLE.
MAREN MORRIS
9781680217964

KANE BROWN
TWO EXTRAORDINARY PEOPLE.
SAM HUNT
9781680217902

KENDRICK LAMAR
TWO EXTRAORDINARY PEOPLE.
TRAVIS SCOTT
9781680217933

NICKI MINAJ
TWO EXTRAORDINARY PEOPLE.
CARDI B
9781680217940

MORE TITLES COMING SOON
SDLBACK.COM/CONNECTED-LIVES